Conquering Your Crossroad Experience

40-day Devotional to Conquer Life's
Toughest Challenges and Obstacles

John F. Miller

authorHOUSE®

AuthorHouse™
1663 Liberty Drive
Bloomington, IN 47403
www.authorhouse.com
Phone: 1 (800) 839-8640

Published by AuthorHouse   07/31/2015

ISBN: 978-1-5049-1930-2 (sc)
ISBN: 978-1-5049-1929-6 (e)

Print information available on the last page.

Any people depicted in stock imagery provided by Thinkstock are models, and such images are being used for illustrative purposes only.

Certain stock imagery © Thinkstock.

This book is printed on acid-free paper.

INTRODUCTION

I was born into a home that loved the Lord. I remember at a young age, going to church many hours during the week praying and serving God. My parents continued asking me, "When are you going to allow Jesus to come into your heart?" I was very reluctant. I truly believe that the Lord saved me because of the prayers and the commitment made by my parents constantly praying for me. When I gave my life to Christ, my life began to be transformed passionately towards Him. My father is a pastor of a church in the area, so my childhood was mostly spent running through the halls of the church on Sundays and Wednesdays and trying not to get caught. In high school, I was involved in the church music ministry. I was a drummer for the choir and worship team. Every time I picked up a pair of drumsticks, my heart was stirred for Christ. After graduating high school, I went to college on a football scholarship. Things were totally different for me than they were back home, and I had to rely on something unique to keep me in line with Christ. I started reading a devotional daily along with prayer. Reading a devotional every day changed my life. It allowed me to make the right decisions, which resulted in God working things out in my favor. During the four years of college, God blessed me with the chance to do the unthinkable and the impossible. I give total credit to God for allowing me to be successful, because of my commitment, consistency and dedication in taking the time to read devotionals daily to see what God was saying to me. The Lord really matured me during the time I spent in college reading. After several years of planning, the Lord called me to write a devotional. This devotional is called *Conquering Your Crossroad Experience – A 40-Day Devotional on Conquering Life's Challenges and Obstacles.*

Question: Want to know how to travel though life's toughest crossroads effectively in spite of life's challenges and obstacles? I'll tell you how I did it. The 40-day devotional that you have in your hand has been designed with you in mind. Its purpose is to recharge, motivate, encourage, discipline, strengthen and restore longevity in you through life's difficult times. The word crossroad takes on a different meaning. Your crossroad experience can be any of the following: relationships, fear, the loss of a loved one, not having friends, can't get a fresh start, never winning, finding love, how to show love, how to fight the enemy, how to be perfect in God's sight, commitment, loving your self, how to be strong in The Lord, patience, progress, distractions, storms, obedience, being devoted, studying God's word, how to follow God's plan for your life, and just simply waiting for God to show Himself worthy. This devotional will help you from start to finish. It's created from relevant spiritual and biblical principles, scriptures and wisdom from God, our creator. Do you remember a time in your life when you desired and sought God's word? Craved and hungered for His presence? Recognized His voice more than ever after or when a storm happens in your life? It's so easy to lose spiritual momentum with God during the most difficult times of your life, but I believe the potential for a recharged, thriving, lasting and reconnecting relationship with God is in this 40-day devotional. It just has to be received, so that a true transformation can begin from a place of fresh surrender to God in the midst of your crisis.

Conquering Your Crossroad Experience: A 40-Day Devotional is designed to help you beat the odds whether it's a challenge or an obstacle. It was also written to detoxify the spiritual mind daily from attacks of the enemy to ensure a healthy spiritual lifestyle before, during or after the problems in your life. The devotional was also created to strengthen your zeal as well as your passion for God in this critical time. Over the next 40 days, read this devotional and incorporate it into your everyday spiritual life. During this 40-day period, don't allow this devotional to leave your sight. Keep it with you everywhere you go; you never know when or where you might need it. Keep it open! Protect and value this incredible time and experience with God.

With reading your Bible, praying and attending church, let this devotional become a lifestyle. I encourage you to establish a frequency and consistency in your life of reading daily. Remember, this is not a legalistic thing. This is an "I get to experience God" thing. It's like taking yourself in for a tune up and an oil change so you can keep your endurance for God and enjoyment of Him at a high and efficient level. I want to encourage you to make it apart of your life.

Acknowledgements

I would first like to recognize the many, many people who believed in me and supported me in every decision in my life. My deepest thanks goes to my Lord and Savior, Jesus Christ. Without him, none of these devotionals would have been published. God has given me the information and knowledge that I am sharing on an increasingly global level. I thank God every day for these unprecedented opportunities of power and faith. I have learned that each individual person has an immense potential for creating who he or she wants to be and become daily.

Thank you for purchasing this unique devotional. I owe a great debt to you for purchasing what God has given me. I can't express the magnitude of the impact this will have on my life and my ministry. This devotional that God has instructed me to write will be an ongoing reminder to me and everyone who reads it to make spending time with God a priority on the ongoing journey through our everyday lives.

Most high regards and thanks to my wonderful wife, Lauren Miller, for supporting me in this great task. You've have been a great friend who has stood by me in the most challenging and difficult times of my life. The strong bond we share, a bond graciously connected by

God, will never be broken, but can only grow as we work together to increase the impact of God's message on the world.

Special thanks to my father, Elder Dr. George A. Miller, who first encouraged and enabled me to write and minister through the gift of encouraging, mentoring and training many years before starting this project. Thanks for being a good example of "practicing what you preached" though the years. I watched you and learned about being a father, counselor, mentor, pastor, published author and trusted friend. Thanks to my parents for equipping me with the opportunity to achieve the American Dream and instilling in me a moral, Christian belief system that would mold me into what God called and chose me to be. Thanks for teaching me enduring life lessons.

Special recognition to my mother, Equilla Miller, who has always pushed me to my limits, encouraging me to become great and express my uniqueness in diverse and colorful ways. Thanks for your matchless support from grade school to adulthood.

Thanks to my family as a whole for being a part of this living legacy that will touch lives for years to come. To my grandparents, George Washington Miller, Annie R. Morris, the late Colbert Turner, Thelma Nash, Montro "Madear" Miller and Alice "Nana" Byrd. Thank you for starting something great by believing in me and for your love and commitment. I will never, ever forget it. Thanks for your faith, patience, wisdom, warm fellowship and especially the homemade hot meals. Until we meet again…

Special thanks and highest regards to my handsome son, Preston Freemon Miller. He has definitely been a blessing to our family. He has really pushed me to do this project. My hope is that this will be something I can hand down to him and that he will one day continue this legacy. As he grows up to be a respectable young man, I will teach him character, excellence, righteousness and love. Thank you, Preston. Without you this idea wouldn't have come forth.

Thanks to all the people in my life in so many places who supported me generously and at times quite miraculously. Deepest thanks to Virginia Gandy, Tina Schotes, Walter Williams Sr., Coach Walter Williams Jr., Coach Enie Watson and family, Opal Wood, Coach Andy Wood, Coach Tim Bell, Coach Ronnie Cuevas, Reginald Castilla, Anthony Miller, Kraven Cook, Willie Legget, Jeremy Johnson, Coach Riley Murray, the late Coach Cleveland Hudson, Coach Willie Totten, Coach Roger Totten, Coach Sam Washington, Coach Bill Lee, Coach Milton Smith, Barrin Simpson, Larry Morris, Tonya Morris, Cynthia Morton, Richelle Keith, Nkechi Chibueze, Wendie Grogan, Nikki Buss, and Coach Fred Clausen.

Lastly but certainly not least, I must acknowledge a dear friend that lost his life unexpectedly. Darryl Butler – You held a great influence and impact on my life. Thank you for being a man of great statue and respect.

TABLE OF CONTENTS

DAY 1

FRESH FIRE BURNING DESIRE

—❦—

*"Never be lacking in zeal, but keep your
spiritual fervor serving the Lord."*

Romans 12:11 NIV

The reminder to keep our spiritual fire implies that we can lose it. Cutting criticisms at work, escalating conflicts at home, and increasing disappointments in life can rapidly deplete your spirit of energy and passion. When the spiritual fire begins to fade, enthusiasm for life begins to die, and can be resuscitated with a prescription or purchase.

The solution for restoring spiritual fervor is found in the great commandment, "You shall love the Lord your God with all your heart and with all your soul and with all your mind." Matthew 22:37 ESV. This is key to conquering your crossroad the best way to rekindle your love and passion for God is to draw closer to Him in your thoughts, words and actions. Start fresh and nourish your spirit by making time to read, meditate, fellowship with other Christians, and share fresh conversations with God. These things will help you keep the flame going strong in your life and deal with the crossroads, and challenges and obstacles that life throws at you. The more we stay fresh in Him, the more He will allow himself to work in our lives.

God will reveal himself in proportion to our burning desire for him. The Christian faith is either fervent or a failure. It is characterized by fire: hearts and lives ablaze, faces glowing with joy, lit with a fervor and love for Jesus. It's my prayer that you join me in this journey to conquer your crossroad experience through the renewed power and burning desire from God.

DAY 2

An Opportunity
To Study?

*And you shall love the lord your God with all your heart,
with all your soul, with all your mind, and with all
your strength. This is the first commandment.*

Mark 12:30 NKJV

Your word is a lamp to my feet and a light to my path.

Psalm 119:105 NKJV

I have hidden your word in my heart that I might not sin against you.

Psalm 119:11 NIV

For many, the word "study" reminds us of unpleasant memories of
hard times in high school or college. We all know studying the Bible
is an important part of developing our relationship with God and

the key ingredient to deal with life's challenges and obstacles. How does studying the Bible help us conquer our crossroad experience?

Think about the people in your life that you truly love. How many of them are complete strangers? How many of them have you only met once or twice? Most of us would say that we love our children, our spouse, our family members (even if we might not <u>like</u> them all the time!), or our close friends.

The point is this: love between people grows out of the relationship they develop with each other. So the way to develop a greater love or passion for God is to get to know Him better. This requires more than a 2-hour service on a Sunday morning or a series of short, "help me now, please" prayers. Any earthly relationship will deteriorate when two people quit spending time with each other. We cannot expect our relationship with God to become or remain passionate if we neglect spending time with Him.

God has revealed himself to us primarily through His word. So if we really want to know Him, we must develop an appetite to read and study His word. The more we read, study and memorize the bible, the more we will know about God. The more we know about Him, the more we will love him, the more he will help us conquer life's most difficult challenges.

DAY 3

SOLITUDE

—❦✿❦—

"In the early morning, while it was still dark, Jesus got up, left the house, and went away to a secluded place, and was praying there"

Mark 1:35 NASB

The practice of solitude is not a retreat from reality or responsibility, but a biblical response to the reality of the demands of numerous duties and activities, the pressure of circumstances, and the many urgencies of the daily routines of life that tend to converge on us all. In the midst of a busy ministry, Jesus established a pattern that teaches His followers a principle that secures balance and helps us retain our priorities. It is important to take time away and focus on positive things in order to beat the odds of your daily challenges.

Simon and his companions searched for Him: they found Him, and said to Him, *"Everyone is looking for you."* Mark 1:36-37 NASB. Life's daily demands and distractions are ever present. Finding times for solitude definitely requires our making a choice. We see this illustration in Jesus' ministry. The practice of solitude was His idea, and it speaks volumes to us today. Normally, people who are able to focus and take quality time to think over things are the ones who are the most successful in overcoming life's crossroads.

When we are alone with the Lord in a quiet quest for God, we are refreshed and reminded how gentle and rich the love of God is and how fully his presence is available if we will give Him time. We do so by withdrawing from other people and pressures so that He can be made known to us!

I pray that you will find a place of sacred solitude that will help you in your daily challenges.

DAY 4

Passion For Peace and Patience

—❦❀❦—

"Wait for the Lord; Be strong and your heart
take courage; Yes, wait for the Lord!"

Psalm 27:14 NASB

Waiting on God peacefully gives perfect time for prayerful reflection, self-examination, and interaction with God's Word. Without this, life and service becomes a blur, often causing discouragement, diversion, or defeat. With this, our lives are continually recharged and restored with energy.

God can work his best in us when we are in a place of peace. When we know that God is going to work things out for us even if they don't look their best, we are showing God that we are fully relying on him to handle our issues and problems. Patience requires us to wait and have peace. Our daily wait time for God to conquer our battles should be filled with peace, prayer, patience and the passion to give our best to the one who saved us.

Growing to know Him means patiently spending time alone with Him to hear His voice and His heart, which brings such renewal in our lives. David understood this, and so must we. There's great power released through reflection and meditation in Christ's presence.

The Holy Spirit will often speak to us in the atmosphere of peace, meditation and patience. *" When you said, Seek May face," my heart said to you, Your face, Lord, I shall seek." Psalms 27:8 NASB.*

Allow heart-to-heart and time to mediate alone with the Lord. Give time to it.

DAY 5

MAGNIFYING: THE LORD

*I will bless the LORD at all times; His praise shall continually
be in my mouth. My soul shall make its boast in the LORD; the
humble shall hear of it and be glad. Oh, magnify the LORD with
me, and let us exalt His name together. I sought the LORD, and
He heard me, and delivered me from all my fears. They looked to
Him and were radiant, and their faces were not ashamed.*

Psalm 34 1-5 NKJV

When I attempt to experience for God to help me conquer my
crossroad and in other areas of my life, I like to go back to the
basics. I think the best way to achieve this is to focus on God. For
me, that means to re-read the Bible, because that is where I have
learned who God is. There is a Psalm that we used to sing that
puzzled me. It says, "Magnify the Lord". Okay "to magnify" means
to make something appear larger than it actually is. I don't think
that is the exact definition that relates here. God is big enough. The
word used can also be translated as "to praise" or "to promote". If
I were translating that verse, I think I would use the word *praise*.

Let me share something I have noticed over the years working in education that relates to the word "magnify" and how we can apply it in our lives. As electrical components get smaller and smaller, magnification aids become valuable tools. And as Christians and believers, magnification of God has gotten smaller and smaller in our daily walk. So let's get back to allowing ourselves to magnifying the Lord daily and not get distracted by the challenges that has to be conquered. When it comes to magnifying the Lord, it is not only beneficial but, also necessary. If we want to experience a victory with God, we not only need to focus solely on Him and lose sight of all the things that surround us. Those things that distract us steal our time and cause us worry. There are a lot of books on God's promises, but I doubt that you find Matthew 6:34 in any of them. In the verse, Jesus promises us that each day will have enough problems of its own.

Let us accept the fact the fact that life will have its own share of problems and concerns, but that should not be our focus. Oh magnify the Lord with me, and let us exalt his name together! Please take a moment and re-read through Psalms 34 in its entirety and as you do ask yourself, "Who is God?"

DAY 6

You Must Clean Out Your Pantry

—❦❀❦—

You shall love the lord your God with all your heart,
with all your soul, and with all your mind.

Matthew 22:37 NKJV

The will to conquer your crossroads in life begins with God and your commitment to our first commandment as a follower of Jesus Christ. This is Deuteronomy 6:5 and Matthew 22:37 NKJV, *"You shall love the Lord your God with all your heart, and all your soul, and with your (entire) mind."* Time and circumstances have a way of pushing what is most important in our lives to the back of the shelf. However, God instructs us to pray and keep his Word ever before us. In Colossians 3:23 NASB, the relationship with God is this; *"In whatever you do, do it heartily as to the Lord and not to men."*

Remember setting up the food pantry in your first new house? Remember how excited you were to all that new, clean space? When we first receive Jesus, we experience that wonderful feeling of being new and clean. We love this new relationship with our Father and have a passion to place the Word of God front and center on the pantry shelves of our minds, so that we can find it quickly every time we open the door. But like the pantry in our home, our spiritual pantry doesn't stay neat and organized. Sometimes, we just quickly unload food items onto the nearest shelf, because we are tired or distracted, sending our favorite snacks not to the back, out of sight and out of mind. We stack more items in front and do not take time to rearrange or move the junk food from in front of the important day to day items that we should be using. It is the same with our mind when the cares of the day start to stack up and keep us from seeing what's best for us, our daily relationship with God.

But if you take a small amount of time at the start of the day to look at your pantry and put a shelf back in order, by the end of the week, the whole pantry is organized and the healthy items are once again front and center. You can do the same with prayer, praise and worship. If you arrange your mind and heart to read from His word each day the beauty of His Love for us, then God will reward your spending time with Him each day by fighting your battles and conquering the toughest challenges that life brings.

DAY 7

STEPS TO RECOVERING YOUR PASSION TO WIN

—❧❀❧—

"Yet I hold this against you: You have forsaken the love you had at first. Consider how far you have fallen! Repent and do the things you did at first. If you do not repent, I will come to you and remove lampstand from its place."

Revelation 2:4-5 NIV

One of the most astounding revelations about our Creator is His passion for His creation. Our God is a passionate God, and because we are created in his image, we are passionate people. God put this wonderful trait in us, so we would be obsessed with Him and His kingdom. However, we live in a sinful world, and the deceiver is always at work trying to divert our passions. Satan doesn't care which distraction you're passionate about, as long as it's not our Savior.

We've all been there, we wake up one day, and we're obsessed with our hobbies. Then something happens that throws us off and causes us to not like what we once did as much. We're not sure when it happened, but somewhere along the way, we lost our passion for our Lord and Savior. Often times when we lose our passion for God, we lose our passion to fight strongly against our crossroads or whatever causes us problems. We tend to give up and not attempt to get better.

A fact about your passion is: it will always tell on you. Whenever you are investing the best part of your life, your passion will always be there. It's simply impossible to separate your passion from your heart.

When you want to conquer the battle of not being passionate for God, look no further than in Revelation 2:4-5 NIV. Jesus is telling the church at Ephesus that they've lost their passion for Him and He explains how to get it back.

Step 1- "Consider how far you have fallen!" Remember how you were when you first received Christ in your heart, you were a walking advertisement for Jesus and His saving grace.

Step 2- "Repent." Ask God to forgive you for putting something or someone else before Him.

Step-3 "Do the things you did at first." Go back to the way you were when Jesus meant everything to you.

Jesus Christ is worthy of all our love, and He wants a passionate relationship with us. Make Him your new hobby, and your crossroad will be conquered again.

DAY 8

PURSUING GOD
TO CONQUER

—❦❀❦—

*"I am the Lord you God, who teaches you what is best for
you, who directs you in the way you should go."*

Isaiah 48:17 NIV

I was having a heart-to-heart talk with one of my mentors. He was
stressing over what he would do with his life. I was encouraging
him that God had the answers; and if he continued to pursue Him,
He would show him the right direction to go and be right beside
him through it all. I explained to him that God had challenged me
to become all that he created me to be, to accomplish all that He
called me to do and to not let circumstances change my perspective.
An example of a circumstance would be any challenge or issue
that would cause us to be thrown off. I began thinking about how
different my life would be today, if I hadn't made the decision to
passionately pursue God's best in every area of my life.

God's desire is to help us receive His best for our lives, but He also asks us to take responsibility in the things we need to do during this process. We must continue to mature in our relationship with God, His word and His ways. Psalm 25:12 TLB says, *"Where is the man who fears the Lord? God will teach him how to choose the best."*

As we humble ourselves before the Lord on a daily basis and seek His will in every situation and circumstance, He will teach us to choose His best every time. Our desires for our lives and our hearts will stay pliable and open to his leading.

Lastly, we must learn to trust Him completely. If we trust God completely, He will serve as our secret service agent and will protect us from any attack, assassination or acquisition that life may bring.

Pursue God to pursue your victory and conquer the crossroads of life!

DAY 9

DO IT FOR THE ONE: LOVE

"Let your light so shine before men, that they may see your
good works and glorify your Father in heaven."

Matthew 5:16 NKJV

We will focus this devotional on the topic that's near and dear to my heart, reconquering a passion for people.

Jesus said regarding the last days, *"Because of the increase of the wickedness, the love of most will grow cold" Matthew 24:12 NIV.* I believe we are living in the most critical time we've ever lived in and experiencing this soul-hardening, family-fracturing, and nation-corrupting tragedy first hand. And in the absence of love, fear and terror increase their reign in a land dominated by a culture obsessed with self and addicted to personal satisfaction.

God wants to see a better response in us, as this is an opportunity to be a radiant beacon of God's love in these critical days.

Here are a few practical suggestions and biblical principles to help you become a more loving person: 1) Repent of personal pride and indifference towards people. 2) Ask God to help you receive a greater dimension of His love and forgiveness 3) Allow the Holy Spirit to guide you to people who need help, hope and healing. 4) Practice being kind in your conversation, humble in your attitude, forgiving in your nature, and gracious in your response. 5) Get involved in local outreach and begin using your gifts and talents in service to others.

As you put these suggestions into action, always remember to pray for those you are reaching out to. Remember the love of God helps us conquer whatever challenges we may be faced with through people. The love of God should be exercised daily so that God can exercise His great victories in us.

DAY 10

WINNERS LOVE TO SEE OTHER WINNERS WIN

"For God so loved the world that He gave His only begotten Son, that whoever believes in Him should not perish but have everlasting life."

John 3:16

This devotion would be referred to as the "love devotion". It is a great definition of love, and yet many of us can honestly say that we do not love with this depth of forgiveness. I don't know about you, but I don't want to be a "clanging symbol". I desire that God's love teach and change me to love more like I Corinthians 13.

God is the ultimate winner of all, because He sent his Son to us to save us from any problems we might face. He wanted us to be winners just like him. Jesus fought the most important battle on Calvary. He died for our sins without a question or a doubt so that we may WIN eternally. God loved us enough to set us up to win.

As we go through our busy lives, we tend to judge people and hold them to a standard that is not realistic. We expect people not to make mistakes. People are going to hurt you and let you down, whether they mean to or not. This includes our friends, co-workers, family members, spouses, our children, and the Wal-Mart cashier, the person who cuts you off while driving, the list goes on and on.

The real story here is how you respond to that hurt and disappointment. Will you be a "clanging symbol"? Or will you walk in the love and forgiveness of our Savior? To truly 'conquer our love for people', we need to accept people the way they are and allow God to change them through His love and grace. Not offer harsh words or a cold shoulder.

Today, as you pray to God to strengthen and conquer your passion for people, remember John 3:16 and that He love us first. If He loves us, then we should love each other.

DAY 11

TRUSTING GOD TO CONQUER ON YOUR BEHALF

"Trust in the Lord with all your heart and lean not on your own understanding. In all your ways acknowledge Him and He will direct your paths."

Proverbs 3:5-6 NIV

We must learn to trust Him completely. It is so difficult to give God all of ourselves. But God is a loving father that wants the good and the bad that we possess in our lives. So many times we feel undeserving; however, God believes in us more than we believe in ourselves.

God works on his time frame. Sometimes he may not work as quickly as we would want Him to but he always shows himself faithful in our times of most desperate need. When we trust in the Lord with all our hearts, God knows that we are in true need of a blessing. He knows we need Him to work a miracle and fight the battle of whatever we may be dealing with. These battles may be relationships, marriages, friendships, issues on the job, problems at church or anything that causes us to stress and doubt our faith.

Jesus wants, not only to be our personal savoir so that we can go to heaven when we die, which is the ultimate victory as a Christian but He also wants to save you in every area of your life. Ask yourself today, *"Just how much will I miss out on in this life, if I fail to pray, believe and trust God for his best?"*.

Today on Day 11, I pray Lord that you will teach us how to desire and pursue your best in every area of our lives to trust you like never before. Remind us that you don't expect perfection, but only cooperation. Thank you that as I refuse to settle for less than your best, you will guide us and guarantee our victory and success to conquer our crossroads. Amen!

DAY 12

THE SMALL THINGS
MATTER THE MOST

—❦—

*"If a man has a hundred sheep and one of them gets lost, what will he do?
Won't he leave the ninety others in the wilderness and go to search for the one
that is lost until he finds it? And when he has found it, he will joyfully carry
it home on his shoulders. When he arrives, he will call together his friends
and neighbors, saying, "rejoice with me because I have found my lost sheep."*

Luke 15:4-6 NLT

It doesn't take long to realize there are great needs in the world. You can read the paper, flip on the news or just notice people as you walk through a public place. There are a lot of people with a lot of needs. There are many people who need the hope that comes from a relationship with Jesus. As we see all these things, it can almost become overwhelming. We can quickly justify laziness by thinking, "with the billions of people in the world, what impact could I make anyway? I couldn't even put a dent in the needs that I see all around me, so why even bother?"

God blesses the people who take the time out to tackle the small things. Any good coach would will tell his team to take care of the small things and the big things will take care of themselves. To conquer life and its challenges, we have to take care of the small things first before dealing with the big things. Each individual person is always important to God. Small acts of kindness are a big deal to the one receiving them and will come out victorious.

I think at times we can have things backwards. Making a massive impact and making headlines is flashy and glamorous, but why not start with loving one friend? Before you move try to feed all of the homeless people in your community, why not start with feeding one? Before you move out of the country to start an orphanage, invite the neighborhood kid who doesn't have a father in his life over to your house for dinner and a game night. If we are willing to start with the "little" and what seems insignificant, do we really need headlines?

The way Jesus operates is different than what we naturally think. The way up is down. The way to doing something significant is at times doing what seems small or insignificant. Lord, help us open our eyes to the small things around us, so you can conquer our big things.

DAY 13

BETTER TOGETHER FOREVER

"And let us not neglect our meeting together, as some people do, but encourage one another, especially now that the day of his return is drawing near."

Hebrews 10:25 NLT

On Sundays, many of us have walked though the doors of a church for many years. What we found on the inside was love and acceptance, a haven from life's storms.

Church for many people was a place where we went to see God touch and change people's lives without knowing that your life would change the most. You see, God performed surgery on me at a young age in church. He opened me up and placed the whole world inside. He gave me new vision and a new heart for people; even though I sometimes strayed away, God always pulled me back towards His will with his powerful hand. I call this transformation "the miracle of me". It's something God does supernaturally in you whenever you give up your name, your desires and your will to follow Him and serve others.

Along with a new heart and vision came a boldness to reach out to other believers as well as unbelievers. Not because I was some great person who thought they had all the answers, but because I had tapped into the tangible source of The One living on inside of me. The One who is the answer, and I wanted to simply share Him with others.

In His word, God tells us *"not to forsake the assembling of ourselves together, as the manner of some is...." Hebrews 10:25a KJV.* Going to church is important. Fellowshipping with others believers is important.

We must stay faithful, encourage one another to be consistent in coming to church, to stay connected to one another through small groups and fellowshipping with other believers. Let's all stay in the fight TOGETHER and let our creator win and conquer our battles.

DAY 14

BACK TO THE BASICS: NEVER STOP PRAYING

Be cheerful no matter what; pray all the time; thank God no matter what happens. This is the way God wants you who belong to Christ Jesus to live.

1 Thessalonians 5:16-18 MSG

Today, many people think of praying as a routine or a task. They assume they have to go to God in a certain and particular way, and if they don't their prayer may not be heard if its not acceptable. But that's so not true. Prayer is the simplest way set forth for us to talk directly to God. When dealing with issues daily, it is important that we get back to the basics of praying a simple prayer to help us conquer every challenge and obstacle we may face. I cannot express enough how much God loves to hear from us and rely on Him daily. So it should be our daily focus to talk to Him throughout our daily lives, and to come to Him in prayer have intimate conversation with him over and over without giving up.

A prayer can be prayed in many different ways. Often times we think that we have to get on our knees and close our eyes all the time, but we can talk to God on the way to work, in between classes, before a game, walking though a dark and unsafe place or anytime. There is nothing against the normal gestures of prayer, but sometimes we are unable to get to a quiet place to pray. So these gestures could possibly keep us away from what's really important – our conversation with God. During the most critical times of our lives, we may not be in a place or position to kneel down and close our eyes.

Finding it hard to talk to God? Write a journal to God. This journal should consist of a list of things that you are thanking Him for, things that you want Him to do in your life and requests for direction on how these things will work in your life. I've been doing this for over 5 years. Journaling has really helped and strengthen my prayer life tremendously. Through my prayer life, God gave me instructions to write this devotional book. Whatever you feel works best for you, do it to the best of your ability. Let's get back to the basics and never stop praying. Never stop talking to God in the difficult times in our lives, and it will change us forever. It is my prayer when you read this devotional today that your prayer life will be strengthened, and you will allow God to take full control of your everyday actions with the basics of prayer. Amen!

DAY 15

PROGRESS VS. PERFECTIONISM

*"Be diligent in these matter; give yourself wholly to
them, so that everyone may see your progress."*

1 Timothy 4:15 NIV

We begin today's devotion by asking God to conquer our passion
for progress. It's God's desire that we make continual progress in
our faith, marriages, family, finances, friends, health and overall
wellbeing. *"Beloved, I pray that you may prosper in all things and be
in health, just as your soul prospers." 3 John 1:2 NKJV*

There's a big difference between perfectionism and progress.
The root of perfectionism is the fear of failure and causes one to
be continually striving to be perfect in order to gain acceptance
and approval from others. Rather than simply doing your best at
something, the perfectionist has to be the best at everything. For

those locked in the performance trap of perfectionism, good is never good enough.

Perfectionism is unhealthy and is a barrier to healthy progress. The perfectionist will will be plagued with procrastination, because the conditions have to be perfect before they began anything.

Progress, however, is rooted in a healthy motivation for continual improvement and is faith-based rather than fear-based. It strives for a spirit of excellence that honors God, inspires people and exalts Jesus. Healthy progress is based on the biblical principle of faithfulness in small things and moving forward with God's process of growth and maturity.

If, like me, you struggle with perfectionistic tendencies, here's some helpful advice. Release your fear of failure through prayer. Be a steady plodder, work with a detailed schedule, surround yourself with people who love you and accept you for who you are. This will help you conquer your weakness and exchange your performance-based tendencies for a healthy, slow-and-steady process towards progress.

Perfectionism hinders performance. Make progress your goal. On earth, *"Nothing is perfect expect God's Word" Ps. 119:96*

DAY 16

RECIPE FOR PROGRESS

"We will be like a tree planted by the rivers of water. We will bear fruit in season. Whatever we do WILL PROSPER."

Psalm 1:3

One of my favorite dishes growing up was my mom's Homemade Macaroni and Cheese. My mom is a wonderful cook. Lauren, my wife, is also a great cook. When she makes my mom's Homemade Macaroni and Cheese, it's as good or better than my mom's, except once. Lauren thought it would be OK to change the recipe (the formula) and put in different kinds of ingredients, thinking I wouldn't notice. But as I bit into a mouthful, it wasn't the same as I remembered. You probably know what my next comment was, "Don't mess with perfection!"

I am not big on formulas when it comes to the things of God, because as soon as we think we've got God figured out, He surprises us in new ways. God's ways are higher than ours. With that being said, His Word can be trusted and the promises therein are "yes and amen."

One of my favorite promises (recipes) is found in Psalms 1. If you are in need of a fresh new outlook for progress and encouragement to conquer your problems, this scripture is just for you. Psalm 1 tells us things not to do, things to do, and the things that are promised. In addition, God gave Moses the greatest recipe that could have ever been given. When God spoke to Moses and delivered to him the 10 Commandments in Exodus 20:1-16 MSG, these commandments were definitely a recipe for good living.

Things NOT To Do: Take council from the ungodly. Stand around with sinners. Sit around with mockers. (Psalm 1:1)

Things To Do: Delight in (a desire for) the law of The Lord. Mediate On God's Word. (Psalm 1:2)

Things Promised: We will be like a tree planted by the rivers of water. We will bear fruit in season. Whatever we do WILL PROSPER. (Psalm 1:3)

If God had anything close to a recipe for progress or victory to conquer, Psalm 1 ist. We would be wise to follow it to the letter. "Don't mess with perfection."

DAY 17

RELYING ON GOD'S STRENGTH TO CONQUER

"Commit your work to the Lord, and you thoughts will be established."

Proverbs 16:3

Have you ever had to face an obstacle in your life that seemed immovable? Or been told news that left you feeling hopeless, and thought 'How do I move forward?' Let's look at a small part of the story of David's life to see what he did when the giants challenged him.

David's job was never glamorous or desired by others, but he still took pride in it and worked to the best of his ability. His greatest desire was to honor God, his Father, with his actions and how he worked. This young man's job put him in the face of a lion but he fearlessly trusted God to deliver it into his hands. This same boy had to fight off a bear to keep his father's livestock safe from harm. But what David did not know is that these test from God, his Father, would prove to him that God was with him whenever he relied on Him. Ultimately, these tests were leading up to a battle with Goliath that would change his life forever. *(See 1 Samuel 17 for the full story.)*

God desires for us to live a life unhindered by the giants we face. This is not to say we won't face these giants, for surely they will come. But when we do face giants, we can rely on God's strength within us. Young David knew from past experiences that God would take care of him, if he put his faith and trust in him. David was unwilling to allow the Philistine Goliath to keep him or the rest of the Israelites from moving forward. When we allow our thoughts to be in line with what God desires for our lives and fully trust Him to accomplish His good plan for us, no giant or crossroad experience is too big to keep us from moving forward in victory in God.

Today, it's my prayer that you allow him to direct your thoughts about yourself, your friends, your family and your children. Focus on His desires for your life and through His strength defeat the giants the enemy puts before you today.

DAY 18

HIS TIMING, OUR FAITHFULNESS, OUR REWARD

"For just as the heavens are higher than the earth, so my ways are higher than your ways and my thought higher than your thoughts."

Isaiah 55:9 NLT

Have you ever wanted something to happen or to be so real that you tried to make it happen on your own timing and power, only to fall short and miss the mark? Now you're left trying to pick yourself up off the ground, discouraged, frustrated, conquered, and even more confused than you were before.

Even though we may have "good intentions", the way we want things to be done always the way The Lord has originally planned to have things done in our lives.

It reminds me of the story of Abraham and Sarah in Genesis Chapters 15-21. Here were two people who served God, loved God and The Lord declared them to be righteous. One day, The Lord appeared to Abraham in a vision and revealed His great plans for Abraham and Sarah's life. A part of that vision was to fulfill a desire within Abraham and Sarah to have a child. Unfortunately the story took a turn when things were not going as Abraham and Sarah thought it should. In our situation, our crossroad experience may not be the issue of trying to have a child, but it maybe waiting on the right job, house, relationship or event to be healed.

Taking matters into their own hands was their first mistake, Abraham and Sarah took the "Ishmael Option". This led them down a path that God originally had never planned for their lives, slowed things down, caused hurt, confusion and started a whole new line, the Ishmaelite's, that never were meant to be in the first place!

Many times in our lives when things are not going as we think they should be going or at the speed we want it to, we hurry along the process only to make things worse than before.

Thank goodness we serve a God who loves us and desires us. According to Genesis 21:2-3, The Lord kept his word and did for Sarah exactly what he had promised. She became pregnant, and she gave birth to a son for Abraham in his old age. And the key phrase here is: *"The Lord kept His word and this happened at just the time God had said it would."* In order for God to fully give us what we desire, we must (first) in all things, submit our lives, our ways and our actions to God to see how He can conquer on our behalf; so that we may come out on top with a victory.

DAY 19

Looking Forward: I
Refuse To Go Backwards

—❦❀❦—

*"Brethren, I do not count myself to have apprehended; but one
thing I do, forgetting those things which are behind and reaching
forward to those things which are ahead, I press toward the goal
for the prize of the upward call of God in Jesus Christ.*

Philippians 3:13-14 NKJV

In Philippians 3, Paul speaks of a "prize" or an "upward call" that
we are to constantly progress toward. Paul compares the entire
Christian life to one big race. One of the biggest adversaries to our
progress is the concept of "arrival". As Christians, we often gauge our
progress according to our victories, failures and comparing ourselves
to others. We must realize that living in the successes or failures
of the past will keep us from looking forward to what's ahead. Of
course, we should celebrate what God has done in our lives. Of
course, we should not move forward if there are areas of our hearts in
need of God's healing touch. But we must realize that God is doing a

new thing and calling us to deeper places in Him. He wants to help us conquer our issues, rejoice with us in times of success, but He also doesn't want us to become stale and stagnant. Maybe you're feeling encouraged by all that you have accomplished during this time. Maybe you're discouraged because you didn't reach a specific goal. Maybe you're looking at those around you and thinking, "They're doing so much better than I am at this." Wherever you are, be encouraged that God has a race laid before you to run. Don't give up! You are not alone! The obstacles that lie in front of you may be different from the person next to you. Look forward and keep your eyes fixed on the prize because the best is yet to come!

During your time of solitude, read Isaiah 43:18-19 and Psalm 139:5. Ask yourself these questions: 1) Have I stopped running my race or given up on reaching my heavenly prize? If so, why? 2) How do I overcome these obstacles and get back on track? 3) What challenges from this devotional has God used to mature my relationship with Him?

DAY 20

LOVE CONQUERS
ALL MISTAKES

"He who covers and forgives an offense seeks love, but he who repeats or harps on a matter separate even close friends. A reproof enters deeper into a man of understanding than a hundred lases into a (self-confident) fool."

Proverbs 17:9-10 AMP

Fifteen years ago, my life was completely and wonderfully changed. I surrendered my life to Christ and accepted Him as my personal Savior. My personal relationship with God began. Although being saved and changing my life started out very exciting, through the years it has been filled with many adventures and challenges. But most of all, it has been characterized by a zealous and powerful love that Christ continued to have for me regardless of my mistakes. We all make mistakes, and no one expects you to be perfect. The most important thing is that we don't keep making the same mistakes over and over again. I use to worry when I fell from grace and went against God's will for my life. And I would ask myself, "Does God still love me?" The answer is yes! No matter how bad I might fall or how bad the mistake is, God still loves me the same and doesn't look at me any different than before. It stems fully and completely from the most awesome and majestic love there is: Jesus Christ. Every day I continue to ask Christ to be the center of my life, my marriage, my family and my walk daily. James 3:17 NIV says " *The wisdom that comes from heaven is first of all pure; then peace-loving, considerate, submissive, full of mercy and good fruit, impartial and sincere.*" In other words, it's God's heart is shown to people when they mess up or when they blow it. Because we all fall short, we should never look down on anyone for their wrong doing. When they sin, when they fumble, when they have faults, and when they fail – it's about what He does for us.

Everything you have in life is a gift from God, even your next breath. If you got what you deserved, you wouldn't be alive. Yet God doesn't give you what you deserve, He gives you what you need: His love, His forgiveness and His grace.

The prayer that I pray daily is: Father God, fill me with your spirit to overflow with your glory. Be a lamp unto my feet and a light unto my path. Teach me to love as you do and help me to always put you first in my life. Give me the faith to love you with all my heart, soul and mind and help me to fervently love my neighbor. You are a great and mighty God. I love you! Amen.

DAY 21

BE PERFECT WITH GOD

—⁖❋⁖—

"Be perfect, therefore, as your heavenly Father is perfect."

Matthew 5:48 NIV

We live in a fallen world, and we are trapped within a fleshly body that desires its own way and its own comfort. Yet Jesus asks us to be perfect, as the Father is perfect. We can also look at scripture and see that our heavenly Father is aware of our frailty, our tendency to sway to temptation (Romans 7:15, Romans 3:10). If no man is perfect, why would Jesus ask us to be perfect?

The Greek word for perfect "perfect" in the passage is teleios. Teleios means "mature, complete, fully-grown, fulfilling our potential". A telos is an end or a purpose. In Matthew 5, Jesus is speaking to the crowd and teaching them about God's character and the blessings that come from walking in His example of mercy, purify, forgiveness, generosity, and love. He is showing them how to love one another and how to keep their hearts right with God. He is showing how to be a light to the world and ends with the words of Matthew 5:48.

So, what is Jesus saying? What does it take to be mature (fully grown), complete or fulfill our potential? Hebrews 12:1 and 2 GNT says, *"….So then, let us rid ourselves of everything that gets in the way, and of the sin which holds on to us so tightly, and let us run with determination the race that lies before us. Let us keep our eyes fixed on Jesus, on whom our faith depends from beginning to end."*

Jesus is asking us to keep looking to Him, to keep our hearts focused on His Word and stay connected to Him in prayer. He will guide us step-by-step and give us the strength and encouragement we need to overcome obstacles in our lives to take our next step. Only with His divine help, we can become mature, complete, fully-grown, and perfect.

Perfectionism is the enemy's trap to sidetrack us from depending upon God. It causes us to become frustrated, critical and bitter. Is there an area in your life or a relationship that you are compelled to try to "fix" on your own? Are you willing to share your feelings of weakness, fear, and doubt with the Lord and ask His forgiveness for trying to accomplish it in your own strength? Jesus wants you to move forward. Are you listening for His voice? Are you to His plan? In your time of solitude read Hebrew 12.

DAY 22

SETTING THE SEED IN
THE WORD TO SUCCEED

—❧✿❧—

*"The farmer plants the Word. Some people are like the seed that falls on
the hardened soil of the road. No sooner do they hear the Word than Satan
snatches away what has been planted in them. "And some are like the seed
that lands in the gravel. When they first hear the Word, they respond with
great enthusiasm. But there is such shallow soil of character that when the
emotions wear off and some difficulty arrives, there is nothing to show for
it. "The seed cast in the weeds represents the ones who hear the kingdom news
but are overwhelmed with worries about all the things they have to do and all
the things they want to get. The stress strangles what they heard, and nothing
comes of it. "But the seed planted in the good earth represents those who hear
the Word, embrace it, and produce a harvest beyond their wildest dreams."*

Mark 4:14-20 MSG

In this particular parable, Jesus gave us some good informative
insight into how He and His kingdom would work in our lives.
When farming, no matter where you are, it's very important that the

farmer knows what to do and what not to do. As a farmer sows the seed, miraculous things happen when seed falls on good, healthy, fertile ground. Our hearts are like the planting field or garden, while the things we are taught are the seeds that grow into the thoughts and feelings that make us who we are. Whatever is planted, whether it's a desirable plant or an unwanted weed, will grow if given the proper nourishment. If we are going to experience all the amazing things Jesus has provided, we must be intentional about planting the "right" things in our hearts and getting rid of the "weeds". Plant His Word, cultivate it and it will produce an incredible harvest. As you fast, expect God to reveal Himself to you more clearly.

On Day 22, I pray, Lord Jesus, thank you for informing me to see the amazing truth of sowing your Word into my life. The harvest that it has produced has transformed my life and has shown me how to conquer in every area of my life. Lord, help me to see you for who you really are. Help me to see myself in light of who you really are. Help me to see myself in light of who I have become because of your gift of forgiveness and righteousness. Amen.

DAY 23

OUTRAGEOUS OBEDIENCE

—❦❀❦—

Samuel addressed all Israel: "I've listened to everything you've said to me,
listened carefully to every word, and I've given you a king. See for yourself:
Your king among you, leading you! But now look at me: I'm old and gray,
and my sons are still here. I've led you faithfully from my youth until this
very day. Look at me! Do you have any complaints to bring before GOD and
his anointed? Have I ever stolen so much as an ox or a donkey? Have I ever
taken advantage of you or exploited you? Have I ever taken a bribe or played
fast and loose with the law? Bring your complaint and I'll make it right."

I Samuel 12:1-3 MSG

The great prophet Samuel gives his farewell address after anointing
Israel's first king. God graciously permitted His people to have an
earthly king and promised to bless them as long as they and their
king remained obedient to Him first. However, the Israelites' failure
to comply with God's standards and instructions resulted in them
missing out on the promises that their ancestors had been graced
with. We must remain obedient to God's instructions, so that he'll
give us what he promised and fight our battles to overcome life's

toughest challenges and obstacles. Obedience is defined as being compliant with an order of instructions (or law) or submission to authority. Being obedient is our way of showing God how much we want to submit our lives to Him, and for God to show us his marvelous acts.

We often struggle with walking by faith and not by sight, so we seek something tangible. God, in His perfect, everlasting permissive will and grace, will grant our requests under a stipulation- that we are completely obedient to His Word. The promises of God always carry the asterisk of obedience. Please read all of I Samuel 12 in your time of solitude.

It is my prayer that God gives me the endurance and strength to be obedient to His instructions. During this devotional, help me hear your voice more clearly so that I can operate within your perfect and permissive will. Amen!

TRIALS, TRIUMPH AND TESTIMONY

—❦❀❦—

As Jesus was getting into the boat, the demon-delivered man begged to go along, but he wouldn't let him. Jesus said, "Go home to your own people. Tell them your story—what the Master did, how he had mercy on you." The man went back and began to preach in the Ten Towns area about what Jesus had done for him. He was the talk of the town.

Mark 5:18-20 MSG

In this passage, the demon-possessed man was struggling with something that not only kept him up all night, it was also something he had dealt with for a very long time. He was in constant agony and wanted relief so badly, which I refer to as his own personal trial. We all have trials in our lives that we want to conquer. The demon-possessed man would cut himself out of frustration, irritation and desperation, wondering why he was dealing with this issue.

Do you ever find yourself so frustrated that you hurt not only yourself, but others as well? Ever struggle to understand why in a particular situation? Notice that in this passage, the man saw Jesus, ran to Him, laid down at His feet and was changed forever. After his remarkable encounter with the Messiah, he was purposely sent back to his hometown so people could see the change that Jesus made in him and his life.

When Jesus brings us out of our trails, He wants us to share our testimony with others. The text mentioned the demon-delivered man which was totally a transformation at a great level because no normal person during that time could control the demon-possessed man. God is capable of doing things supernaturally in your life, causing you to conquer with triumph and share our testimony with others. During your time of solitude read all of Mark 5.

Today, on Day 23, I pray that we would have the kind of passion it takes to lay all of my burdens on to Jesus. I am faced with many different challenges and issues, and I know God cares about every single one of them. Thank you God for caring about every single detail of my life. Create a testimony through my experiences that will reach others and bring you the glory you deserve. Amen!

DAY 25

DARE TO BE DEVOTED

—⚜—

Samuel called the people to assemble before GOD at Mizpah. He addressed
the children of Israel, "This is GOD's personal message to you: "I brought
Israel up out of Egypt. I delivered you from Egyptian oppression—yes,
from all the bullying governments that made your life miserable. And now
you want nothing to do with your God, the very God who has a history of
getting you out of troubles of all sorts. "And now you say, 'No! We want a
king; give us a king!' "Well, if that's what you want, that's what you'll get!
Present yourselves formally before GOD, ranked in tribes and families."

1 Samuel 10: 17-19 MSG

During today's devotion, I want to address a very important
quality of the Christian believer. Being devoted. In 1 Samuel 10,
Saul was clearly appointed by God as Israel's first king and leader.
As a result and the release of the Holy Spirit's work in Saul, he
became a different person. *"Saul turned and left Samuel. At that*
very moment God transformed him—made him a new person! And
all the confirming signs took place the same day." 1 Samuel 10:9 MSG
God was everything and more of what Saul needed for success to

lead his people and to be a great king, but as Saul's power grew, so did his pride. During this time Saul stopped seeking God's will, and eventually jealousy and strife began to decay both him and the nation he had been entrusted and appointed to lead.

During the times in our lives when we are successful and have conquered the odds, we have to make sure that we stay DEVOTED to God and His will for us. Lets not get distracted by the people, position and place that God has elevated us to when we have success.

Our success depends solely on our devotion to God, not our position, wisdom, or strength. God honors obedience. We must consistently obey and devote ourselves to God. Rebellion and disobedience against God and His will for us is a very dangerous sin. As we choose to rebel, we lose the forgiveness and restoration we have with God as He intervenes to conquer on our behalf. Please read 1 Samuel 10 to its entirety.

Today, I acknowledge that God is my everything and that I will DEVOTE every area of my life to His service. I will continue to ask for forgiveness for sins of any kind, whether it be disobedience, arrogance or rebellion to God's word. On Day 25, I will render control to God and ask the Holy Spirit to fill me so that I might live a life that glorifies God.

DAY 26

Seeing, Struggling and Surviving Your Scariest Storms

Late at night, the boat was far out at sea; Jesus was still by himself on land. He could see his men struggling with the oars, the wind having come up against them. At about four o'clock in the morning, Jesus came toward them, walking on the sea. He intended to go right by them. But when they saw him walking on the sea, they thought it was a ghost and screamed, scared out of their wits.

Mark 6:47-49 MSG

We all know the story in Mark 6, when Jesus walks on water to comfort all 12 disciples. After reading the passage one thing that stands out to me is that Jesus never takes His eyes off of His disciples. Though He may not have been with them in the boat in that moment of the storm, it didn't mean that He wasn't aware of everything that was taking place during the storm.

Naturally, when we may find ourselves in the scarcest storm of our lives we call out to Jesus for help. If Jesus doesn't show up in the very instant we want him, it doesn't mean that He doesn't see us or that He doesn't know or care where we are. It means He wants us to see where we are, to recognize that even in storms that are no match for us, he can and will save us. Though it may feel like you are alone in your boat during your storm, you can rest assured in the knowledge that the Savior always has His eyes fixed on us and would never let us sink.

Today on this 26th day, I am declaring that I will trust in God to a greater degree to save us from the scariest storms of life. I acknowledge that you have all power and that your eyes will never leave us. I thank God for the assurance of knowing that He will conquer my strongest and scariest storm.

DAY 27

YOUR CHOICE VS.
GOD'S WILL

—❧❀❧—

*"What have you done?" asked Samuel. Saul replied, "When I saw that
the men were scattering, and that you did not come at the set time, and
that the Philistines were assembling at Mikmash, ¹²I thought, 'Now the
Philistines will come down against me at Gilgal, and I have not sought
the LORD's favor.' So I felt compelled to offer the burnt offering."*

1 Samuel 13:11-12 NIV

In 1 Samuel 13, it was no surprise that Saul was truly stressed and
under a lot of pressure to lead the people into battle. Though he had
been given very specific and detailed instructions on how to proceed
and conquer, he felt compelled to offer the burnt offering himself
instead of worshipping in the Lord's way as he had been instructed.
Saul had a choice, but he chose to as he saw fit. Even though Saul
couldn't see the effects of his decision at the time, it was a huge
mistake that cost Saul the anointing as king. In order for God to
fight our battles, we must always follow His will and His way. No

matter what your instincts might be telling you, it's never an option of the Holy Spirit to go outside of God's will to get things done. As leaders, respected by many, if we do not follow God's plan, we run the risk not only of removing ourselves from God's will and protection, but also everyone we have the privilege of leading.

During the most critical times in our lives, let us make the right choice which is God's will. Let us choose God's way to lead our marriages, families, children, friends and everyday associates. Read 1 Samuel 13 and ask yourself, What is God saying to me?

Father, I thank you for the instructions you've given us to follow that allow us to conquer. When we make these choices to follow obediently the Holy Spirit will guide and prompt us in your most matchless ways. Help us to always choose your way over our own ways for your ways are higher than ours will ever be. Amen!

DAY 28

HOW TO PREPARE FOR
YOUR PROBLEMS

After arriving back home, his disciples cornered Jesus and asked,
"Why couldn't we throw the demon out?" He answered, "There
is no way to get rid of this kind of demon except by prayer."

Mark 9:28-29 MSG

After reading Mark 9, I noticed a very particular situation. The
disciples found themselves unprepared to deal with a problem that
they felt they should have been able to manage. Because the twelve
disciples followed and worked with Jesus so closely, they were
challenged with the fact that they could not deliver the demon out of
the boy. Jesus led a lifestyle of prayer and preparation. He didn't wait
until the problem arose to prepare. Daily, He kept Himself ready for
warfare though the power of prayer. Prayer is the key element that
Jesus used to prepare for problems. As Christians, prayer should be
essential to our daily lives. Just as we groom we groom ourselves
daily in order to look presentable in front of everyone we come in

contact with, so should we spend time in daily prayer in order to be prepared for whatever we may face.

Prayer prepares us for what lies ahead. We don't have to wait until we have an issue to start praying the prayer of emergency. We can just simply pray for basic things until God blesses us. Let's not disrespect God and only pray to Him when we have our problems. Let's prepare ahead of time in prayer so when we are confronted with adversity or challenges, we can face them head on.

On day 28, I say to you let us set time aside to pray and seek God. In prayer we are strengthened, prepared, and filled with His word in order to conquer any issue that may come in front of us. God knows exactly what we are in need of before we even ask for it. We will forever thank God for His grace that enables us to face whatever lies ahead. Read all of Mark 9 and ask yourself what God is saying to you?

DAY 29

OVERCOMING OPPOSITION

—❦❀❦—

*But David got wind of Saul's strategy to destroy him and said to Abiathar the priest, "Get the Ephod." Then David prayed to G*OD*: "God of Israel, I've just heard that Saul plans to come to Keilah and destroy the city because of me. Will the city fathers of Keilah turn me over to him? Will Saul come down and do what I've heard? O G*OD*, God of Israel, tell me!" G*OD* replied, "He's coming down."*

1 Samuel 23:9-11 MSG

David was surrounded by opposition his whole life. Even though he knew he was about to be betrayed in verse 9, he still prayed and worshipped God. Worship and prayer are powerful together. No matter how hard the opposition is, prayer overcomes opposition and prayer also enhances our daily wellbeing. In the end, God came though for David. David found himself separated from his enemies, delivered from danger and resting in the stronghold and safe place of En-gedi.

David's life was overwhelmingly filled with trails and challenges. At times, he was running for his life just to survive. At other times, he was hiding out in caves just to protect himself and have solitude with God. It was a constant battle. But there were two things that remained throughout the legacy of David's entire life: worship and prayer. David already knew deep down within his heart when it came down to it- regardless of what he went though- that was all he needed to overcome and conquer.

Throughout this devotional, you have been establishing a consistency of reading God's word, as well as worshipping and taking time for solitude with God. Please let's remain consistent, recognizing that this is the lifeline to strength and the only way to overcome any opposition, adversity, or challenge in our lives.

Read all of 1 Samuel 23 to see what God says to you personally.

DAY 30

SERVITUDE

Whatever you do, work at it with all your heart, as working
for the Lord… It is the Lord Christ you are serving.

Colossians 3:23-25 NIV

Today's devotion deals with serving. Serving is another daily trait
that we should practice to get closer to God. As Christians we should
essentially give ourselves up in servitude. Serving others around us
is very important to us in our walk with Christ. Serving says to
the Lord that we are passionately seeking to help others and not
ourselves just as Christ did in the Bible. *" The Son of Man did not
come to be served, but to serve…" Matthew 20:28 NIV.* One purpose
that Jesus was given when he came to us on earth was to serve, shown
here in Matthew 20:28. He always served in some capacity, whether
it was teaching, preaching, healing, feeding the hungry, praying or
simply loving.

"I am among you as the one who serves." Luke 22:27 ESV In this passage the Apostle Paul is sharing about serving others. He had a deep passion to serve. Paul believed that serving someone should be like pouring out the last drops of your life to someone to help them. The deep passion that Paul used to serve others was shown through the blessings of God granted to Paul. Serving others is like serving God. When we serve His people He will love us and bless us more. Loving to serve His people is what God wants in our lives. The more we serve, the more He loves us.

Serving is not always the most pleasurable thing to do. Christ died on the cross to ultimately serve us. Jesus had to deal with the persecution and violent acts committed against him. Jesus loved us enough to die for us while we were separated from God by sin. Lastly, serving is our personal way for us to show our greatest love for God, through exhaustively helping to build His people, love His people, motivate His people, and devote our lives to make us stronger to conquer life's challenges.

DAY 31

FORTUNATE FRIENDSHIPS

―❧❀❧―

So Jonathan made a covenant with the house of David, saying, "May the LORD call David's enemies to account." And Jonathan had David reaffirm his oath out of love for him, because he loved him as he loved himself.

1 Samuel 20:16-17 NIV

Jonathan said to David, "Go in peace, for we have sworn friendship with each other in the name of the LORD, saying, 'The LORD is witness between you and me, and between your descendants and my descendants forever.'" Then David left, and Jonathan went back to the town.

1 Samuel 20:42 NIV

In I Samuel 20, the Bible covers a very important topic – the friends we choose to be close to us. Our friends make an impact on a lot of our decisions and help us in a lot of ways, that we overlook. In order for us to handle life and the challenges and obstacles that come with it, we must surround ourselves with friends that will push us, encourage us and keep us in a place of wanting to seek God's Word.

David was really fortunate to have a friend like Jonathan. Jonathan was a friend who stuck by him through thick and thin. Jonathan was a friend that would even feel a righteous anger because of the shameful treatment David received. In other ways, Jonathan was a diehard friend to David, the kind of friend he needed very much during this time in his life. Consider it a task of yours to find friends in your life that will be a friend to you just like Jonathan was to David. Jonathan was unselfish; he cared about David's wellbeing consistently, and made an account to God over David's enemies.

What kind of friends do you have? We must strive to have friends in our life like Jonathan – the ones who will encourage and support us, no matter what. In addition, we must always be willing to to be a 'Jonathan' kind of friend to others as they are to us.

On day 31, we must remember to surround ourselves with people that will always point us towards our best. Today we seek God in helping us make the right decision to choose our friends and for God to reveal these friends to us. All in all, God, help us to be the people you called us to be through friendships.

DAY 32

DISCONNECTING FROM DISTRACTIONS

When they come from the marketplace they do not eat unless they wash. And they observe many other traditions, such as the washing of cups, pitchers and kettles. So the Pharisees and teachers of the law asked Jesus, "Why don't your disciples live according to the tradition of the elders instead of eating their food with defiled hands?"

Mark 7:4-5 NIV

In this text, the Pharisees and teachers of the law had been given the commandments and instructions to follow the structures and teachings of God. But along the way, the Pharisees and teachers somehow have gotten distracted. They seemed to have missed the whole point. Their perception and adaptation of the law had become empty, confusing, hollow, and heartless.

Distractions are a big part of why God doesn't fully work in us, because he doesn't have our full attention. The Pharisees and teachers were completely thrown off and distracted by a simple human tradition shown in these verses: *and saw some of his disciples eating food with hands that were defiled, that is, unwashed. ³ (The Pharisees and all the Jews do not eat unless they give their hands a ceremonial washing, holding to the tradition of the elders. ⁴ When they come from the marketplace they do not eat unless they wash. And they observe many other traditions, such as the washing of cups, pitchers and kettles. So the Pharisees and teachers of the law asked Jesus, "Why don't your disciples live according to the tradition of the elders instead of eating their food with defiled hands? "Mark 7:2-5 NIV* Sometimes we get so caught up in routines that we forget what God can do for us and through us with his power. The simple issue here is the disciples did not wash their hands before they sat down to eat their food. This was clearly a teaching by the Pharisees of a human rule. When we bless our food before we eat, it's our way of showing God that we fully trust Him with the task of blessing what maybe unclean. It's easy to settle into a routine and focus on doing things on a schedule and a to-do list. Although we don't mean for it to happen, often times the voice of God gets ignored by simple distractions. Let's stay focused to tend to the regular patterns of life in God's way, not our own. Please read the entire passage of Mark 7.

Dear God, as we choose to disconnect from all distractions that are thrown at us, we vow to get closer to you in every area of our lives. Please let our eyes be steady on what you have given us through prayer and meditation. Help us now so that we won't allow ourselves to lose focus on the things of substance. Amen!

DAY 33

THE DAVID AND GOLIATH EXPERIENCE

—⁂—

As the Philistine moved closer to attack him, David ran quickly toward the battle line to meet him. Reaching into his bag and taking out a stone, he slung it and struck the Philistine on the forehead. The stone sank into his forehead, and he fell facedown on the ground. So David triumphed over the Philistine with a sling and a stone; without a sword in his hand he struck down the Philistine and killed him.

1 Samuel 17:48-50 NIV

In this particular text, Saul was a seasoned warrior. If anyone knew which weapons would be more efficient to conquer and defeat Goliath, it was Saul. God wanted to deliver His people in a way that would leave no doubt or question about what He had done in this David vs. Goliath challenge. It was clearly a situation where God would have to show His strength through David. By using a shepherd boy with a small stone and a sling, God made sure no man would be able to take credit for David's victory over Goliath. In our lives, there may be big giants or big issues that may require God to show Himself for us to receive victory through Him. These issues I would call our "Goliath Challenges". They would be the following: losing a job, financial troubles, disagreements with loved ones, depression, life-changing decisions, and getting closer to God. The "Goliath Challenges" would have to turned over to God completely for Him to fully conquer through us.

When we rely on our own strength, we will experience personal limitations. But when we trust fully in God's power and strength, He will bring us to a victory like none other. He gets the victory and the glory, and we get to be a part of His great plan.

We have all heard the saying, "It's like bringing a knife to a gun fight". In Mark 17:38-39, it states - *Then Saul dressed David in his own tunic. He put a coat of armor on him and a bronze helmet on his head. David fastened on his sword over the tunic and tried walking around, because he was not used to them.* After that David didn't like his army clothing so he took them off and wanted to go without them. Instead, he chose five smooth stones from a stream and a sling. David really felt the boldness and the power of God at this moment. That power carried over into the battle in which David conquered Goliath. Read the entire 17th chapter of I Samuel to view what God says to you.

DAY 34

FEAR < LESS: FIGHTING FEAR TO CONQUER

David took these words to heart and was very much afraid of Achish king of Gath. ¹³ So he pretended to be insane in their presence; and while he was in their hands he acted like a madman, making marks on the doors of the gate and letting saliva run down his beard.

I Samuel 21:12-13 NIV

In today's devotion, I want to touch on the word "FEAR". In this passage David is running from Saul and, for a short period of time, is overcome by fear. At this moment, David is at a very low point in his life. He acts like a crazy man before the King of Gath. The interesting thing about this situation is David was fearless when he faced Goliath (the giant), but now David has let fear take over before the King of Gath. David was beyond the point where he needed help; he was simply experiencing a bad episode of fear. He let fear control him. Any one of us can be subject to fear at any point in our lives. When we experience fear, the best thing for us to do is pray and read the word of God to seek what He every area of our lives. There are many things that could make us afraid. We should pray daily about these things so that God will allow us to overcome fear in those areas. Sometimes when we give in to fear, it is because we are tired, or hurt, physically and mentally. When we are at our lowest, it is hard to believe we can achieve what's ahead of us. The only way to fight fear is with the word of God and prayer to conquer whatever is causing fear in our lives. God can give us back our courage, the same courage that David had in 1 Samuel 17 when he defeated one of the tallest giants of his time. In order to ensure we don't start doing wrong things and going places we should avoid, we must remain deeply rooted and connected to God. His love and passion for us will cast out any level of fear no matter how big or small. As a Christian, the only person we should fear is God. The person who fears God the most loves God the best.

Do not be afraid of them; the LORD your God himself will fight for you. Deuteronomy 3:22 NIV To sum it all up always remember Deuteronomy 3:22 NIV. We should never fear anything, anyone, anywhere, or any situation because God will fight and conquer for us.

Dear God – Help us manage our lives so that we may be filled daily with the spirit of boldness and faith, and to be fearless. Amen!

DAY 35

COMEBACKS ARE POSSIBLE

—⊙❀⊙—

At this, Job got up and tore his robe and shaved his head. Then he
fell to the ground in worship and said: "Naked I came from my
mother's womb, and naked I will depart. The LORD gave and the
LORD has taken away; may the name of the LORD be praised." In
all this, Job did not sin by charging God with wrongdoing.

Job 1:20-22 NIV

After Job had prayed for his friends, the LORD restored his fortunes and
gave him twice as much as he had before All his brothers and sisters and
everyone who had known him before came and ate with him in his house.
They comforted and consoled him over all the trouble the LORD had
brought on him, and each one gave him a piece of silver and a gold ring.

Job 42:10-11NIV

We all know the story in the Bible of Job and how God gave Satan
permission to touch and effect Job's possessions and all the things
that had an earthly value. Every time I read the book of Job, it

takes on a different meaning. God gave Job this challenge because he knew Job could handle it. Job 1:8 MSG says *GOD said to Satan, "Have you noticed my friend Job? There's no one quite like him—honest and true to his word, totally devoted to God and hating evil."* This was definitely a true statement from God saying that he trusted Job and that he could handle this task. So God gave Satan permission to move forward and do what he wanted with Job's things, but he could not touch Job.

It's very clear that God was in control of this situation, because he gave certain instructions to Satan on what he could and could not do. Please remember whatever challenges and obstacles we have, God is always in control of it all. After Job received all the messages about the tragic things that started to happen and the things that were taken away, Job stayed focused and got to his feet, ripped his robe, shaved his head, then fell to the ground and worshiped: *Naked I came from my mother's womb, naked I'll return to the womb of the earth. GOD gives, GOD takes. God's name be ever blessed. Job 1:21 MSG* Even after all those things were taken away from Job not once through all this did Job sin; not once did he blame God. He continued to be faithful, righteous, and remained resilient.

Lastly, God accepted the prayers from Job and granted his request. God completely restored everything that had been lost. God even gave Job double of everything he had lost. This is a true testament of a comeback. Job showed resiliency and for his faithfulness he was rewarded. Job lived on another 140 years, living to see his children and grandchildren—four generations of them! Then he died – an old man, with a full life. Be strong and God will conquer your toughest challenges and obstacles for you, just like he did for Job.

DAY 36

RESILIENCY

—❧❀❧—

Now Saul feared David. It was clear that GOD was with David and
had left Saul. So, Saul got David out of his sight by making him an
officer in the army. David was in combat frequently. Everything
David did turned out well. Yes, GOD was with him. As Saul saw
David becoming more successful, he himself grew more fearful. He
could see the handwriting on the wall. But everyone else in Israel
and Judah loved David. They loved watching him in action.

1 Samuel 18: 12-16 MSG

In my own words, being resilient would be one of the characteristics
of David. Resilient means being able to recover from or adjust easily
to misfortune or change. Clearly, David overcame more than his
share of setbacks, from facing a giant with only a sling and a stone
to having Saul try to kill him. In I Samuel 18, though Saul tried
to kill David, he eventually recognized the hand that God had on
his life. David's life was full of challenges, battles, fear; betrayal,
fighting a giant, trials, obstacles, hiding in caves, adversity, stress,
and lack of support. Through all of these things David continued to

be blameless before God in spite of all his challenges. David's success and favor came in two stages. First, David understood from his past experiences that his success was a result of the Lord being with him. Second, David was given the responsibility of leading the king's men into battle against the enemies of Israel. David had determined in his heart to advance the kingdom regardless of how hard it would be to take the job. In the end in verse 30 the text says that David's name was on everyone's lips because God was with David. This is a true sign of resiliency.

During today's devotion reflect on the victories that God has given you in your life and consider them as preparation and confirmation of the victories to come, so you will be able to show resiliency through Christ. Praise God for what He has delivered you from. God has positioned you in your life to commit to Him and advance in the kingdom of your King, Jesus.

Thank you Father, for all that you have done, and the way you have helped us during our trying times. It is in you, that we do all the things that we are allowed to do here on earth. Help us to acknowledge you and receive your grace in everything that we do. Allow us to continue to be resilient and bring glory to your name as you empower us to advance your kingdom. Amen!

DAY 37

CONQUERING
COMPROMISE

—❦❀❦—

*So Nahash went after them and prepared to go to war against Jabesh
Gilead. The men of Jabesh petitioned Nahash: "Make a treaty with us
and we'll serve you." Nahash said, "I'll make a treaty with you on one
condition: that every right eye among you be gouged out! I'll humiliate
every last man and woman in Israel before I'm done!" The town leaders of
Jabesh said, "Give us time to send messengers around Israel—seven days
should do it. If no one shows up to help us, we'll accept your terms."*

1 Samuel 11:1-3 MSG

In this particular passage, the Israelites were under attack. Was there
anyone that could save them? As I looked further in this text, I found
some interesting symbolism in this chapter. Nahash is defined as
"serpent." Jabesh is defined as "dried up." The "eye" is symbolic of
sight and vision and whenever "right" is mentioned, as in the "right
hand of God," it symbolizes power and authority. When, I read
chapter 11, clearly, the attack was not only physical, it was ultimately

a spiritual one. When our walk with God is compromised, we start to feel disconnected from Him. Also when our relationship with Jesus feels "dried up", our enemy launches his strongest attack. Often times, this is when we experience our greatest challenges, obstacles and defeat, when the power of our relationship with our creator dries up. I defined "dried up" as lacking something needed or being depleted of essential daily needs. Let's make sure our marriages and our relationship with God are not "dried up", so that God will give us spiritual clarity and the ability to endure compromise.

Have you ever in your life considered compromise as an option? Compromise comes from lack of vision and authority over the enemy. Today, I ask the Holy Spirit to reveal any compromise in your life and where you need to be recommitted and "un-dried up" in your walk with Christ. Respond and recommit in obedience and Jesus will restore both your authority and your vision so you can conquer compromise in every area of your life.

As we desire to commit to following God with all our hearts, we must remain "un-dried up" in our walk with our Lord and Savior. When we are in tune with God, we will be able to see any compromise, intentional or not, that may creep in. We have the vision and authority to conquer all. Please read all of 1 Samuel 11 to see what God is saying to you.

DAY 38

CHOOSE TRUST OVER FEAR

—⟡❀⟡—

When I am afraid, I put my trust in you.
In God, whose word I praise—
in God I trust and am not afraid.
What can mere mortals do to me?

Psalm 56:3-4 NIV

We all have issues with fear. I describe fear as **F**rantic **E**ffort **A**void **R**eality. When we are in fear we are not ourselves. We are often in a frantic place when we are afraid and this causes us to lose interest in the things that we once loved doing or had a passion for. We also try to avoid places, people, and things. And lastly, we try to avoid reality. David blocked all of these things but yet he trusted the one who deserved his trust, God. In this particular passage, David decided to put his trust in God when people were attacking him. He asks, "What can mere mortals do to me?" This rhetorical question is really a strong declaration of confidence in the God he serves.

What a way to show genuine trust and faith and freedom from fear of an earthy man.

Proverbs 29:25 says, "The fear of man brings a snare." The enemy knows how to scare us with snares and tricks. We have to be strong enough to fight off every snare that the enemy throws at us. A good way to do this is to always call out the things that we are in fear of just like David. David just simply stated, "What can mere mortals do to me?" as a sign of his trust, that God had his back.

God wants us to place our trust in Him and fear only Him. Not be afraid of Him, but have a healthy respect, esteem, honor and loyalty to the Lord. When the Lord holds this place in our hearts and minds, we don't have to be afraid or have fear of any other man. We've all heard the saying that faith and fear can't live in the same house. That's just what God is saying to us in this passage.

Today, as you have read this devotion, let's make sure when we are afraid of others or their opinions, that we choose to trust in God. Let's also only fear God and honor Him with esteem above all others. Once we do these things, He will give us freedom from fear.

HIDDEN BLESSING'S IN THE STORMS OF LIFE

As soon as the meal was finished, he insisted that the disciples get in the boat and go on ahead to the other side while he dismissed the people. With the crowd dispersed, he climbed the mountain so he could be by himself and pray. He stayed there alone, late into the night.

Matthew 14:22-23 MSG

I can't think of anyone who enjoys storms or anyone who would volunteer to go through one, but one thing is for sure: we can learn a lot from a storm. Storms are natural and they are part of God's earthly desire. When you look at storms from a scientific approach, storms are created when warm, moisture- laden air rises quickly into the atmosphere causing precipitation to fall and strong, rapid winds to take to take over. Many people think storms are bad; however, storms are necessary for individual growth and progression of faith.

In this particular passage in Matthew 14:22-23, Jesus sent the disciples ahead to go get on the boat to go back to the other side of the shore. Jesus had just finished a great miracle when he fed 5000 people from five loaves and two fish. Jesus wanted to finish up so he sent the disciples ahead so he could go pray in solitude that night in the mountains. Jesus sent the disciples out on the water for a great reason. Why wouldn't Jesus get in the boat with the disciples? I think Jesus wanted the disciples to go though a storm for there own good. So when we go through storms we are in good company.

We can still be in the will of God and still be caught in a storm. There is always a purpose and a plan for the storm that God puts in our life. Storms are God's means for transportation. When God moves us to the next level in our lives he requires us to go through a storm so we will know that we are strong enough and that He is with us forever. God will never keep us from our storms; he will always keep us in the midst of the storm. He is always there waiting to rescue us at the right time in the storm. *Psalms 34:19 NIV says, "The righteous person may have many troubles, but the LORD delivers him from them all;"*

Storms also refine us into stronger individuals. We should use our storms to rebuild our faith and make it stronger than before we had the storm, and to be more like Jesus Lastly, storms are God's means of testimony. When God brings us out of the storm, it should be all the more reason for us to share with others what He has done for us in our life. Remember Jesus is the master of the storm and when He wants us to go through it, we will come out blessed.

DAY 40

BIG GOD, BIG VICTORIES, WITH NO LIMITATIONS

Jonathan said to his armor bearer, "Come on now, let's go across to these uncircumcised pagans. Maybe GOD will work for us. There's no rule that says GOD can only deliver by using a big army. No one can stop GOD from saving when he sets his mind to it." His armor bearer said, "Go ahead. Do what you think best. I'm with you all the way."

1 Samuel 14:6-7 MSG

In Samuel 14, Jonathan and his armor bearer made room for God to act on their behalf. They had the understanding and perspective that God was bigger than them and able to do more than they could ever do. They also understood that God did not have the same limitations, setbacks or hindrances that they were subject to.

In the most difficult season of your life you should make room for God in your life through every aspect and means available: praying, sharing your testimony, reading God's word, meditation, loving your enemies, redefining yourself, desiring to follow God, having self-discipline to remain consistent, being dedicated to work you believe in, reflecting daily in solitude, having faith, and proving the power of God through the success and victories He has won in your life. When we make room for God and make Him available in our lives, we allow God to operate in every area of our life. He can do much more to fix our situations than we can. When we fully submit all the areas of our lives to God, He can remove the hindrances and push past our personal limitations.

On the last day of this devotional, I request that we ask God to show us the areas of personal limitations in our lives. We know that God wants to bring a big breakthrough for us in this area of our life. I pray that God will show us how to make room for Him to make big moves in our lives. Show us, teach us, guide us, and change us for the better. Dear Father God, you are bigger than we are and you can do way more than we can do! Amen!

I pray this 40-day devotional has blessed you as it has blessed me. Please continue to pray, practice and place these devotions in your life. Please share with others and make it a daily routine. Be Blessed.

IN CONCLUSION

I want to encourage you to be just as intentional about the next forty days… and the forty days after that…. And so on. Remember, keeping the fire and zeal for God burning in your heart is what will allow you to continue to conquer every crossroad in your life, and it will keep your relationship with Him fresh and new. It will allow you to continue serving and obeying Him from a position of want to, and you will experience the joy of salvation every day, regardless of what life brings your way. The basic principles you have practiced in these forty days are very easy to sustain long-term. Prayer, solitude and personal devotion are quite simple to incorporate into your everyday life. Over these last forty days, you have created space for God to fill. The best way to continue in these same practices is to keep that space open indefinitely. Don't allow it to close up! Protect that time and space with God and make it your priority each day.

Just like reading your Bible, praying, and attending church, reading daily devotions is also a lifestyle. I want to encourage you to establish a frequency and consistency of praying and reading God's word in your life. Remember, this is not a legalistic thing. This is an " I get to experience God more and more daily" thing. It is like going into heaven for a tune up, so we can keep our passion strong for God and our enjoyment of Him at a high level. I encourage you to do the same. Figure out what works for you. Commit to it, and make it a part of your life. Be blessed. Love you immensely.

About the Author

John Miller is a uniquely qualified, humble young man with a young voice for his generation that God has ordained to serve His people through honor and integrity. Through insightful words and creative concepts for youth ministry, mentorship and education, he displays a passion to serve others like there's no tomorrow. A second-generation minister, John was born in Jackson, Mississippi and raised in Starkville, Mississippi. Growing up, John developed a love for helping people and building relationships at a young age. His heartfelt passion for people led John to become a teacher and educator to help students and teenagers as he was helped growing up. He currently works as an educator/middle schoolteacher in McKinney, Texas, where he teaches middle school history and social studies. It's very clear from his childhood that the hand of God directs his life. He is known for teaching, serving, and mentoring at all costs. He uses his unique skill set to aid in the up building of a sure and stable organization within the community of faith. He is committed to making a positive difference in the lives of people and is passionate to see them developed and empowered.

John Miller's spiritual journey began in July 1997 when had a personal experience with Christ.

Throughout his Christian experience, he has served in various capacities. Growing up under the leadership of his father, Eld. Dr. George Miller, he served as a church musician. After graduating college and moving to the Dallas area, John served as pastoral support and youth pastor/director at Praise Fellowship Center under the leadership of Pastor Larry Dyer in Little Elm, Texas. John is currently working with Restoration Fellowship Church as a leadership team member. John is also a licensed minister. John has truly enjoyed working in these extremely powerful churches learning the in's and out's of ministry.

Supporting the vision of those whose lives he touches with humility and grace, John's work in mentoring and working with teen's shows his passion for people that will create an everlasting ministry in his life. This passion has allowed him to work with many of the prominent ministries across the southern region of the United States, networking to learn more about successful urban ministry. Whether ministering himself or assisting others, it is clear to most that this man is a catalyst for change.

John has made it his ministry to mentor young men of all ages. Presently, John proudly uses each of his experiences at both failing and succeeding as opportunities to teach others what to do and what not do do, showing young people how to use failures as second and third chances to reinvent themselves into living purpose driven lives. John is a great example for young men and a friend who helps educate young men to become men.

When he is not ministering or assisting others in ministry development, he enjoys a wide range of hobbies and interests. His hobbies range from golf to football to fashion, from custom home painting to educational politics. His fashion sense has enabled him to do fashion design for many of his co-workers, peers and fellow laborers of the gospel. From faith to fashion, from education to ministry, John Miller continues to remain relevant in ministry. To be sure, he has captured the intrigue of all those who have been exposed to his gifting and grace.

John completed his associate's degree in 2006 with a concentration in secondary education from Holmes Community College in Goodman, Mississippi, where he earned a scholarship in football. John also earned district recognition in football for his position as an offensive lineman with the NJCFA. He completed his undergraduate studies in 2008, earning a Bachelor of Science degree in Health/Recreation and Secondary Education from Mississippi Valley State University in Itta Bena, Mississippi, where he was also a member of the football and golf teams. He lettered in football and earned an honorable mention award in the 2007 football season. In 2010, he also received his master's degree from Texas Woman's University in Kinesiology with a concentration in Management and Sports Administration.

Through his education, ministry experience and interests, he not only wants to better his community, especially the lives of men, he also seeks to bridge the gap between faith and the "real world" so that others can learn, lead and live more cohesive and authentic lives. With excitement, humility and power, John Miller is anointed to be a leader in this generation and help change a new era in God that is filled with purpose, faith, humbleness and power. John believes he is deemed to save others mentally and physically and help them realize how to be worthy and value God. Growing up, John adopted his motto from a popular inspirational song: "If I can help someone as I pass along, if I can cheer somebody with a word or poem, if I can show somebody how to live through the way I live. Then I'll know my living was not in vain". His goal is to usher young people into the presence of God so that a true relationship is produced.

He is a man after God's heart and he ministers and serves every day like it's his last, with an unparalleled level of intensity and emotion. He lives by the motto "Only what you do for Christ will last." John Miller and his committed wife, best friend and partner in ministry, Lauren Miller, have one beautiful son, Preston Freemon Miller.